Ohio Postcard History

Lawrence County

Terry L. Baldridge

GreenAlva Publishing

Dedication

To my good friends in Lawrence County Ohio.

Copyright © 2022

Terry L. Baldridge

www.terbald.com

ALSO BY TERRY L. BALDRIDGE

Eastern Kentucky Railway

Images of America *ASHLAND*

Huntington Then & Now

Ashland, Huntington, Ironton & Portsmouth Through Time

COUNTRY LINES WORDS & PHOTOS

Raceland, *Eastern Kentucky Horse Racing History*

Greenup County *Kentucky Postcard History*

Boyd County *Kentucky Postcard History*

Won't You See That I Get Justice?
(The torture and murder of Mary Magdalene Pitts)

Thank You!

I would like to thank my family for their kind support. My wife, Heather, who puts up with my sitting for hours reading and writing in my study. She also travels with me to explore archives, libraries, and to help me with photographs as required. She is that special someone who is eager to be at my side no matter what life's weather condition is like. My son, Keenan, and his wife Bethany, who are always willing and ready to support both set of parents. I would like to thank the Lawrence County Public Library, the Boyd County Public Library, the Greenup County Public Library, the Huntington, Ashland, Ironton, and Portsmouth Facebook History Site. There are many more out there that inspire me and help me along. **Romans 14:19**

CONTENTS

1	Introduction/Postcard History	1
2	Lawrence County	6
3	Ironton	7
4	Birds Eye Views	9
5	Bridges	12
6	Businesses	20
7	Cemetery	28
8	Church	30
9	Clubs	33
10	Courthouse	35
11	Downtown	38
12	Floods	47
13	Fun Cards	50
14	Hanging Rock	53
15	Homes & Streets	56
16	Hospital	61

CONTENTS

17	Hotel	62
18	Iron	65
19	Lake	70
20	Parks	73
21	Rail	77
22	River	79
23	Schools	87
24	Tunnel	90
25	Gallia County Ohio	93
26	Jackson County Ohio	96
27	Scioto County Ohio	99
28	Boyd County Kentucky	102
29	Greenup County Kentucky	105
30	Cabell County West Virginia	108
31	Wayne County West Virginia	111

Introduction

I received my first area postcard around 1975 or so. It is a black and white photograph postcard of an Eastern Kentucky Railway engine on a turntable at Grayson Kentucky. It was the next best thing to having the actual tangible railway to me. I had seen a photograph or two of this particular railway in a newspaper, but to own a piece of history was exciting. Up until that point, this railway was just verbal stories and an article to read here and there.

According to postcard historians in the United States, there are several historical phases postcards have gone through and therefore, they are divided into eight categories.

Period	Years
Pre-Postcard Period	1848-1870
Pioneer Period	1870-1898
Private Mailing Card Period	1898-1901
Post Card Period	1901-1907
Divided Back Period	1907-1915
White Border Period	1915-1930
Linen Period	1930-1945
Photochrom Period	1945-Present

Postcard History

The Pre-Postcard Period cards were not cards at all, but envelopes engraved with a picture of some sort. At that time these were referred by many as "mailed cards." In 1861, John Charlton copyrighted the first postcard in America. It was that same year that Congress passed an act allowing private printed cards weighing one ounce or less to be sent in the mail.

In 1870, Hymen Lipman, the man who first patent the pencil with an attached eraser, began issuing his own "Lipman's Postal Cards." Thus began the Pioneer Period. In 1872 Congress passed another act that approved government production of postcards. One side of the postcard was for a small message while the opposite side was for the recipient's address. The government issued cards back then cost one cent to mail and the privately printed card doubled that amount at two cents!

The Private Mailing Card Period came about because of a great deal of public complaining. After yet another congressional act, privately produced postcards cost the same as government issued cards to mail. It cost one cent to do so. There was a difference on the private mailing cards than on the government cards. It was a simple statement, "Private Mailing Card."

Introduction

By the end of 1901, private printed cards were allowed to replace the private mailing card with "Post Card." However, like the old private printed cards, writing was not allowed on the address side of the post card. So, if a person wanted to add a small sentence or a few words to the recipient, they had to write on the front image or message side. Some historians refer to this time as the Undivided Back Period.

The Divided Back Period began with a meeting of Congress in 1907, which allowed for privately produced postcards to divide the back of the cards. The left half for messages and the right for the address. This is also known as the "Golden Age of Postcards." Many local businesses in small communities produced postcards to promote their business or communities. Many of these postcards were real photograph cards. This is what my Eastern Kentucky Railway Engine postcard is. These types of cards became very popular during this time.

The White Border Period saw the availability and popularity of postcards fall. Germany led the world in postcard printing technology and quality. It was their well printed cards that people would purchase and use. However, when the United States entered the Great War

Postcard History

and fought with Great Britain and France against Germany, the postcard printed presses stopped producing. Instead, the United States began to produce all the postcards at this time. As a result of producing poor quality products, popularity fell. Factor in this equation, the shortage of paper and ink, then it is easy to understand why the "Golden Age of Postcards came to an end. But this is not the reason this period is called the White Border Period. This came about to save ink, printers printed up to a certain space from the edge thus leaving a small white border around the card.

The Linen Period came about because of the high fiber or rag content in the printing process. This caused the cards to look like they were printed on linen. Many of the postcard characteristics of the past such as white borders were incorporated into this process. The newer technology also allowed adding descriptions of the image into the white border area below or above the image.

The Photochrom Period began after the end of World War II and continues today. It is a color or black and white photograph printed on a postcard front. It's that simple! Many people today are familiar with this postcard as they are available today.

My Collection

In 2007 Boyd County Kentucky historian James Powers showed me his tristate postcard collection when we were working on a photo history book of Ashland. I could not believe how extensive his collection was. He had hundreds of postcards of the tristate area as well as other cities of Kentucky.

This in turn motivated me to see what cards I have and what specifically would I like to collect. I'm from Argillite in Greenup County Kentucky, so I chose to collect Greenup County postcards primarily however, my collection has extended to other local areas, such as the tri-state area of Kentucky, Ohio, and West Virginia.

It was back in 2008 that Jim asked me to scan his hundreds of area cards. This I did over a couple of month period. I gave him a digital copy and I kept one. The cards in this book are from several sources including my collection.

Jim passed away in the late summer of 2020. Per his wishes, his collection was broken down and sold. So, some of the cards in this book have now passed onto others who enjoy collecting these little historical postage pieces of the past.

Who knows, perhaps one day you will purchase a unique local postcard from the past that once belonged to Mr. Powers!

As selfies and social networks continue to grow in popularity and convenience, the day of using postcards have ended. I hope this book will serve as a reference reminder of how people from Lawrence County took pride in various facets of their lives and wanted to share that pride in the form of a postcard, a message, and a stamp.

Lawrence County

The early history of Lawrence County is similar to many of the river counties that come together in the Kentucky, Ohio and West Virginia area.

Lawrence County was formed from Gallia and Scioto counties in 1816 and has a total area of 457 square miles. It is the southernmost county in the state of Ohio and is surrounded by the Ohio counties of Gallia, Jackson, and Scioto. At that time, Burlington was the seat of county government.

The first white settlers in the area were the Kelly and Keyser families and they settled at Hanging Rock.

Lawrence County was part of the Hanging Rock Iron Region which included several counties in Kentucky. More iron furnaces were located in Lawrence county than any other in the region.

There are many postcards featuring Lawrence County. Unfortunately, there are very few or no older postcards featuring subjects outside of Ironton and Hanging Rock. If any become available at a future date, I will update this book with them.

Many areas in Lawrence County were stops along the Underground Railroad. These areas included homes in towns, farms, stores, iron furnaces and other places. Former slaves from the south were provided food and shelter during these stops on their journey north into free Canada. Many prominent Lawrence County abolitionists took the lead when it came to assisting men and women on their way to freedom.

Ironton

Ironton was founded in 1849 on the banks of the Ohio River. The original town was between Etna Street and Vernon Street and from Seventh Street south to the Ohio River. The land size was approximately 400 acres and cost $17,692. The town was founded by the Ohio Iron and Coal Company. The man behind this purchase was the company's president, John Campbell. The city would elect its first mayor, James M. Merrill in 1851. Over the preceding decades, Ironton would outgrow those original acres to the extent we see today.

The iron produced at furnace sites were shipped to Ironton where it was manufactured into an iron product or loaded at the wharf unto barges for easy river transport to markets east and west. It was the heart of the Hanging Rock Iron Region and Campbell's town flourished.

During the mid 1800s, Ironton's iron production was one of the foremost in the world. To get iron produced by the furnaces to that world wide market, the Iron Railroad laid track from the Ohio River to near Washington Furnace north.

Ironton was host to two major railroads. The Detroit, Toledo and Ironton Railroad and the Norfolk and Western Railway which took over the old Scioto Valley Railroad. Both constructed depots in Ironton.

A postcard photograph of John Campbell near the end of his life. Campbell was born in Brown County in 1808 and worked his way up through the early iron industry. He died in 1891.

Clearly, the city was centered around the iron industry and nearly every business and public services had a link to it. But there were very few Ironton postcards highlighting the iron industry or public services. Thankfully, I have several that will be included in this publication and if more are found in the future, they'll be added to an updated version.

Not long after Ironton became a town, leaders formed the first city school. It began in 1849 at the home of Burnadine Blake on Front Street. From that time to the present, Ironton has made the education of its young citizens a priority with safe and updated structures.

Entertainment in many forms has graced the city since the 1860s. Parks, rock formations, baseball, semi-professional football, school activities, movies, dances, and the list continues.

Though Ironton is no longer the Iron Producing city of the past, the people look back with a great deal of pride at the cities history with an eager anticipation of what the future will bring.

Birds Eye Views

   Birdseye view postcards of cities and places of interest provided just that, what it would look like from a bird's perspective.

   Birdseye Postcards of Lawrence County were much easier to do for the illustrator and the photographer as the cities are surrounded by hills. Climb a hill in either direction and draw or photograph to your heart's content. For unknown reasons, very few of these postcards were produced of Ironton and not one is known to exist of other towns in the county.

This view comes from near the Park Avenue Tunnel area of Ironton. The postcard dates from around 1910.

A 1908 postcard view of Ironton looking north toward the Ohio River.

This view with the Ironton Russell Bridge is from around 1930.

BIRDSEYE VIEW OF IRONTON, OHIO   E-1023

A bird's eye view of Ironton looking from east to west.

Bridges

Lawrence County had quite a few covered bridges spanning creeks along several routes. The covered bridges are gone and no postcards of them are known to exist. But we do have quite a few postcards of the Ironton Russell Bridge and the N&W Railroad Bridges which spanned the Ohio River between Kenova, West Virginia and South Point, Ohio.

The Ironton Russell Bridge was opened in 1922 and was demolished in 2017. The first Norfolk and Western Railroad Bridge was a single track structure with wide piers and began service around 1892. It was rebuilt as a two track structure and went into service in 1913. It continues to be used today!

Norfolk and Western R. R. Bridge across Ohio River, near Ironton, Ohio

This postcard from around 1905 depict the original N&W Railroad Bridge from 1892. As the demand for West Virginia's coal increased, the bridge was rebuilt as a two track bridge and opened in 1913.

The Fallie assist a large barge with navigating the piers of the old N&W R.R. Bridge in this color postcard from 1909.

A bird's eye view of Catlettsburg shows the newer N&W R.R. Bridge in profile. The bridge was rebuilt and opened to rail traffic in 1913. This postcard dates from the 1930s.

Three bridges crossing Ice Creek. This postcard from 1915 shows two N&W R.R. Bridges on the left and the Third Street Bridge on the right.

This postcard shows early construction of the Ironton Russell Bridge from around 1920.

14

Top: A view of the Ironton Russell Bridge from around 1922. Note the wooden deck with construction equipment lining the two lane structure.

Bottom: A black and white photograph postcard of the bridge with Russell in the foreground.

The following three pages: Miscellaneous Ironton Russell Bridge cards range from photograph postcards to hand printed color prints. The years these were printed are from the early 1920s to the 1940s.

Ironton Russell Bridge, Ironton, Ohio

15

IRONTON-RUSSELL BRIDGE, IRONTON, OHIO

BRIDGE OVER OHIO RIVER, FROM RUSSELL, KY.
Photo by - Frank Dowdy, Jr., Russell, Ky.

IRONTON-RUSSELL BRIDGE OVER OHIO RIVER   IRONTON, OHIO

THE IRONTON - RUSSELL BRIDGE
Photo by Stewart

17

Scene on Ohio River, Russell and Ironton Bridge, Ironton, Ohio
2A354-N

Russell-Ironton Bridge, Russell, Ky.
1A125

A color view of the Ironton Russell Bridge from the 1930s. Note Ironton's skyline in profile.

This postcard photograph view shows the Kentucky hills above Russell in the background as well as some of the Norfolk and Western Railroad Depot below center.

Businesses

An unknowable number of businesses have come and gone within Lawrence County throughout its history. During the early days of its existence, the county was a world wide leader in the manufacturing of iron therefore, many supporting business operated throughout the county.

Lawrence County does have some postcards that were produced to highlight local businesses however, it doesn't have nearly the amount of postcards produced by businesses in the Ashland, Huntington, or Portsmouth.

This early postcard photograph is of the old Ironton Post Office at the corner of Center and Fourth Streets.

Along with the post office, several businesses shared this building. This 1905 postcard points out that the building was the Odd Fellows Temple.

This is a postcard view of the Ironton Post Office not long after moving to the Fifth Street location.

This is a 1907 postcard of the old City Water Works that was located next to the Ohio River.

A color postcard view of the old Excelsior Shoe Company building with main offices.

22

This color postcard view of the Excelsior Shoe Company shows the great size of the factory. Because their shoes were offered at lower prices, the company avoided a fiscal setback during the Great Depression.

This postcard of the Selby Shoe Factory shows a great deal of the 1920s Art Deco Style in its construction.

23

Cigar Factory, 3rd & Vernon Sts, Ironton, O.

Many area women were employed by the Swisher Brothers Cigar Company. This five story structure served as one of their branch factories for many years. This postcard dates from 1913.

An early indoor postcard view of the Goldcamp Furniture Store. This postcard dates from the early 1920s.

A PLEASANT PLACE TO SELECT YOUR HOME FURNISHINGS.

MODERATE PRICES—GOLDCAMP FURNITURE STORE, IRONTON, OHIO. HIGH QUALITY.

OFFICE OF O'KEEFE & CO., UNDERTAKERS, IRONTON, OHIO

A 1930 photograph postcard view of the O'Keefe & Company undertakers office.

A public services postcard of the Ironton reservoir and filtration plant. Very few postcards such as this were produced.

CITY RESERVOIR AND FILTRATION PLANT, IRONTON, OHIO.

Above is a color postcard view of mourners of President McKinley gathering around Memorial Hall in 1901.

A 1905 photograph postcard view of the Grand Army of the Republic Memorial Hall.

A 1960s spring view of Ironton's Memorial Hall entrance. The hall was used as the city hall and as an American Legion for many years. It was demolished in 2014.

A 1940s view of the Ironton swimming pool. Ironton High School and Tank Stadium are in the background.

Cemetery

Ironton has several cemeteries across the city, but only Woodland Cemetery seems to have printed postcards advertising their beautiful surroundings. According to several sources, the cemetery dates back to 1870 and today contains more than 29,000 interments.

Along with Ironton's founder, John Campbell, are the remains of many prominent citizens. Foremost for me is the grave of Nannie Kelly Wright, the lone female Iron Master of the region and possibly the world.

The Little White Bridge, "When the Snow Flies", Entrance to Woodland Cemetery, Ironton, Ohio News.

In Beautiful Woodland Cemetery, Ironton, Ohio

Vault in Woodland Cemetery, Ironton, Ohio

Church

Religious services in the area can be traced back to the very early times of Lawrence County. Almost every iron furnace community as well as other county villages had a church which serviced as the center of activity.

Those services in Ironton began as the streets of the city were being laid out. Many churches within the city can trace their beginning to over a century ago or more. Several churches produced postcards to promote their congregations as well as to highlight the architecture of their meeting structures.

This postcard of the Congregational Church is from around 1917.

The three postcards pictured are from around 1920 and gives us a glimpse of the streets and surrounding buildings of the time.

31

A 1910 postcard view of the gothic looking Spencer M. E. Church building.

The bell tower and clock stand out in this Fifth Street view of the Presbyterian Church from 1916.

Clubs

Ironton has been and is home to many associations, unions, and clubs. The Elks, Moose, Masons, Steel Workers, Y.M.C.A, Boy Scouts, Girl Scouts, American Legion, as well as many others have been fixtures of Lawrence County for many years.

I have included the postcards of clubs from the past that is in my collection presently. If more become available in the future, I'll add them to a later edition.

This postcard dates from the early 1930s and shows the Ironton Elks Lodge on Park Avenue. The structure is a mixture of Art Deco and Greek Revival and is one of my favorite designs in the city.

Pictured are two early 1920s postcards of the Masonic Temple at the corner of Center and Third Streets. This building was constructed after the Masonic Opera House was destroyed by fire in 1915.

Courthouse

The first courthouse in Lawrence County stood in Burlington which was the county seat beginning in 1816. The seat of government was moved from Burlington to Ironton in 1851. The courthouse used at that time burned in 1857 and another structure was used as the courthouse until the early 1900s.

The construction on the current Neoclassical courthouse began in 1906 and was completed in 1908. The design of this courthouse is reminiscent of the style Thomas Jefferson used in many of his construction projects.

Pictured is a hand-colored 1910 postcard view of the courthouse from Fourth Street.

COURT HOUSE, IRONTON, LAWRENCE COUNTY, OHIO. Compliments of S. G. Gilfillan, Ironton, O.

The top photograph postcard dates from around 1920 and was clearly done during the winter months.

The color postcard to the right is from 1925 and shows the Ironton Courthouse with the flag blowing in the wind.

The three postcards on page 37 show the courthouse from the 1910s to around 1920. Note the color of the dome was done in brown in the last postcard view.

Lawrence County Court House, Ironton, Ohio.

36

COURT HOUSE   IRONTON, OHIO

Court House,
Ironton, Ohio.

New Court House, Ironton, Ohio.

Downtown

The downtown layout of streets have changed but little since John Campbell's day. Buildings and businesses have come and gone along with generations of people however, many characteristics remain. Much of what was captured in these postcard views are recognizable today.

Many photograph postcard views of Center, Second, and Third Streets were produced between 1903 and 1930. In this publication, views of churches, clubs, and homes near the downtown are in other chapters of this book.

Wagons line the courthouse side of Center Street looking south in this 1911 photograph postcard view of downtown Ironton.

A familiar look back in this color postcard view of the intersection of Center and Fifth Streets.

This 1910 postcard view of Center Street demonstrates the changes that particular portion of downtown Ironton has experienced over the past century.

This 1912 photograph postcard view of Center Street looking south. This postcard was printed by the Ironton Book Store.

This 1910 color postcard shows the Spencer Church steeple and residence on the corner.

This 1910 postcard view of Center Street demonstrates the changes that particular portion of downtown Ironton has experienced over the past century.

A horse and buggy stop in front of a shop at the corner of Second and Adams Streets. The postcard dates from about 1909.

An Ironton streetcar is visible in this Second Street photograph postcard from 1913. Note the intersection street lamp.

This is a very rare night view of Ironton's Second Street. These postcards were hand painted to look night from photographs taken during the day time.

Another street car view of Second Street. Automobiles have taken the place of horses in this 1921 postcard view.

This color postcard view show a busy day on Second Street. A 1920s city bus is pulled over to the left.

The flood of 1907 was highest the river had reached since 1897. This postcard view of that flood on Third Street gives us a glimpse of just how far the river reached then.

The Hayward Block contained the 5 & Dime Store along with several business on Third and Center Streets. This postcard is from around 1910.

Looking from Center Street along Third Street in 1910. The Hayward Block is on the right.

This postcard view from the early 1930s show the growth experienced from the time of the previous postcard. The old Marlow (labeled Harlow) Theater is to the left and J.C. Penny on the right.

A South Third Street is busy with automobiles and flags in this late 1930s postcard view.

We have another view of the first flood of 1907. Third Street and the Hayward Block is on the left. Men and boys look toward the rising water as it creeps along Center Street.

Floods

The first flood photograph postcards of the area date to the flood of 1907. Several postcards were produced using old photographs from 1884 and 1897 but most flood postcards were produced after the floods of 1913 and 1937.

Like every other surrounding county, Lawrence County has experienced significant Ohio River flooding. Most notable are the floods of 1832, 1847, 1884, 1913, 1937, and 1944 because they reached or exceeded the 60 foot mark.

Surprisingly, there were very few flood photograph postcards produced regarding Ironton. Just a few that I can find, and I've shared two them in the previous chapter. I have only five to share in this little section.

The destruction left in the wake of the 1913 flood is evident in this photograph postcard from the period. That flood reached just above the 67 foot mark.

Ironton, Ohio News.
High Water (58 feet) Ohio River (1901), Ironton, Ohio.

Several gather at the old Ironton Wharf to look at the rising Ohio River. There are no records that indicated the river reached 58 feet that year. It did reach 53 and this may be a misprint.

A boat transports a couple of men along an Ironton street in this photograph postcard from 1913. Cold temperatures made assisting others more difficult during that record flood.

Residential areas near the river fall victim to the nearly 68 foot flood of 1913. Many old wooden structures were either destroyed or weakened because of this historic flood.

The flood of 1937 reach just over 70 feet and was the largest flood to occur in the area. The flood wall that was completed in 1942 was designed to protect the city during a flood of similar levels.

Fun Cards

Many humor themed postcards were printed in the early 1900s. The actual photos were taken elsewhere and sold without words to local vendors such as drug stores and jewelers.

A customer would purchased the postcard and have their desired phrase or place added by the vendor. These postcards have been very popular from the beginning of the 20th Century through today. Though today they come with the wording preprinted on the card.

The following Ironton fun cards date from the early 1910s to the early 1920s. They depict humorous themes but can also be used to convey a message that all is well or "I've been busy".

Moving to Beautiful Ironton, Ohio.

Rustic Scene near Ironton, Ohio.

Sulphur Springs, near Ironton, Ohio.

By the Road Side with no Gasoline, near Ironton, Ohio.

Travelling on a "Hoss" car, in "Old Kaintuck", near Ironton, Ohio.

An Illustrated Fish Story, Ironton, Ohio

Hanging Rock

The village of Hanging Rock was named not because of the sandstone cliffs that seemed to hang over the Ohio River, but for a large section of rock that fell into the river.

It was that rock along with the river's current that would hang up or ground the flatboats and early river boats. That rock was referred to as hanging rock and eventually the name was adopted by the small village.

The village was close to the geographical center of the greater area iron producing counties of Northeastern Kentucky and South-central Ohio from the early 1800s to the early 1900s. Therefore the area was called the Hanging Rock Iron Region.

This is a 1915 color postcard view of the Hamilton Iron Furnace which stood between the Ohio River and the tracks. The furnace was built in 1886 and was also known as the Hanging Rock Furnace.

Hanging Rock Furnace near Ironton, Ohio.

A late 1910s view of the Hanging Rock Furnace in Hanging Rock. The furnace operated into the later 1920s, however by 1930, the furnace had blown out and had been dismantled.

This 1909 postcard view is of the old Hamilton Iron Furnace company store that was across the tracks from the furnace. The building housed not only the general store but the company offices and depot as well.

Store and Office, and N. & W. Depot, at Hanging Rock, near Ironton, Ohio

NEAR IRONTON, OHIO

HANGING ROCK AND LOG CABIN POST OFFICE AT HANGING ROCK   E-1029

Many still remember the old Hanging Rock Post Office which was located in a log house. This postcard view is from around 1950.

Homes & Streets

According to several early maps of Ironton and Lawrence County, many street layouts have changed very little. Some roads have experienced changes due to traffic requirements but many still follow routes that have existed for decades.

Lawrence County has many old stately homes that are well over a century old. This chapter contains several postcards depicting scenes of Ironton's Park Avenue as well as Fifth and Sixth Streets.

This is a 1915 postcard view of a city map of Ironton. Most major cities produced postcards such as this in the early part of the 20th Century. Often the sender would circle their location on the map which served as directions when the family member or friend visited. The next several pages contain postcards from the 1910s to the early 1930s of homes along popular streets in Ironton.

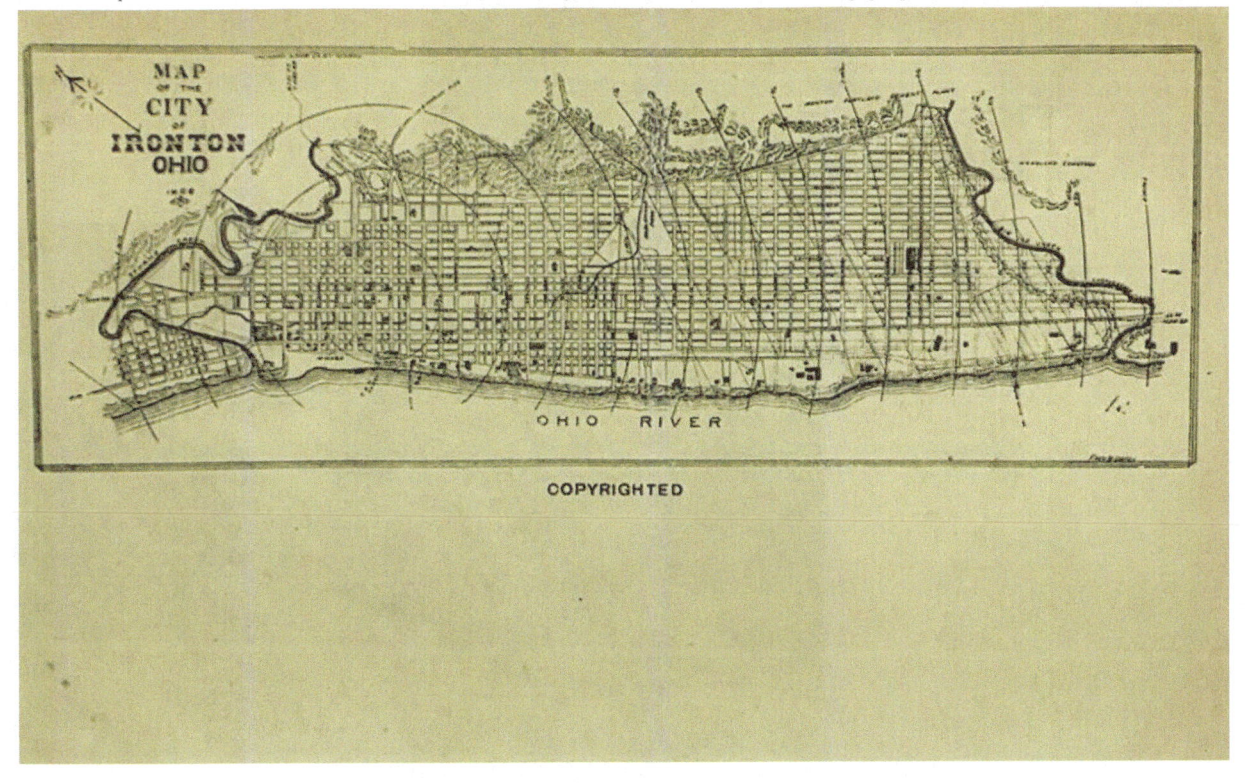

Looking down Park Avenue from Fourth Street,
the N. & W. Depot in the distance, Ironton, Ohio

View on Park Avenue,
Ironton, Ohio.

View on Fifth Street, Ironton, Ohio.

Presbyterian Church, Fifth Street, Ironton, Ohio.

Fifth Street above Vernon St, Ironton, Ohio.

5th St., Looking North, Ironton, Ohio.

Looking down Fifth Street (Snow Scene) from above Park Avenue, Ironton, Ohio.

"Ironton, Ohio News".

Sixth Street, near Adams, Ironton, Ohio.

SIXTH STREET LOOKING EAST

Hospital

Hospitals in the early 20th Century produced and sold postcard views of their facilities in great quantities. This was a way to advertise their impressive buildings in color.

Ironton's Keller Hospital produced a couple of postcards during the 1910s. The hospital was located on Fifth Street and named after Dr. Lester Keller. Keller would sell the facility to Dr. William F. Marting in 1914. By the mid 1960s, the building had been converted to apartments.

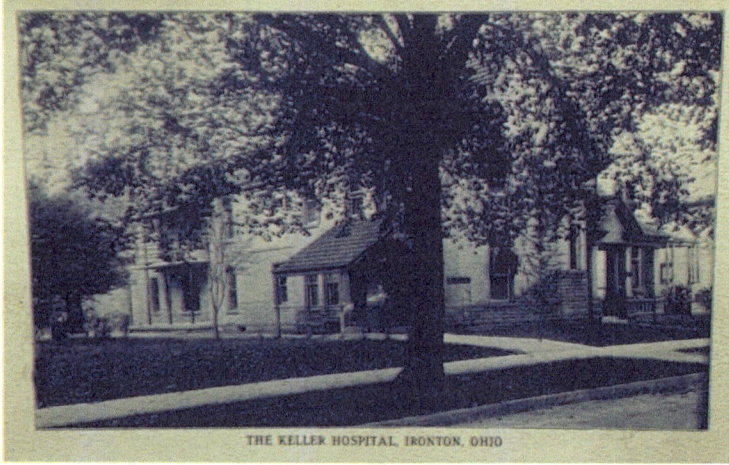

Hotels

Hotels have used postcards to advertise their services for decades and the hotels in Ironton were no exception.

The Marting Hotel produced several postcards throughout it's early history. It was called one of the best hotels in the Ohio Valley during it's heyday.

The hotel was constructed in 1917 and changed ownership over the years. At one time, the Marting and Ashland's Ventura Hotel were owned by the same group. The Marting Hotel building now serves as a beautiful apartment complex for senior citizens.

A 1925 color postcard view of the Marting Hotel and the Marlow Theater on Park Avenue.

A circa 1920 postcard view of the Marting Hotel at the corner of Park Avenue and Second Street.

A 1940s view of the old Lyle's Tourist Home along 52.

This is a 1960s postcard of the Lyle Motel in Ironton. The motel was owned by Gene and Marge Moeller from 1975 to 1985.

This is a 1970s postcard view of the Don Keys Motel in Coal Grove. Many today remember the good times and food while staying there.

Iron

The history of iron making in the area can be traced back to the first charcoal furnace in the Hanging Rock Iron Region. That furnace was Argillite Furnace in Greenup County, Kentucky and it began working in 1818.

The first furnace in the region on the Ohio side of the river was located near Hanging Rock. It was the Union Furnace and it began producing iron in 1826. From that time onward, Lawrence County would claim more iron producing furnaces in all of the Hanging Rock Iron Region and perhaps the state with a total of 15 charcoal iron furnaces.

There are very few postcards of these older furnaces as the majority of them had gone cold long before the postcard age.

John Campbell's Vesuvius Furnace was built in 1833 and was the first furnace in the country to employ a hot blast oven into it's iron production in 1837. This postcard dates from the 1940s.

The Buckhorn Furnace was built in 1834 and blew out in 1884. Part of the old stack is the only thing remaining today. This postcard was printed and distributed in 1935.

The Howard Furnace operated from 1853 to 1881 in Scioto County Ohio. This postcard is from 1935.

This 1918 postcard view of Ironton shows smoke from a couple of a couple of iron mills near the Ohio River.

This rare color postcard of Big Etna Furnace is from the 1920s. .

Lime Stone is a vital ingredient which acts as a flux in producing iron. This is a rare postcard view of a local lime stone mine.

Charcoal supplied the heat for melting the ore and lime stone. Below is a postcard of a Ironton charcoal warehouse.

An evening time view of the old Union Furnace Mills.

Another view of the furnace stack that once was Vesuvius Furnace. It is located at Lake Vesuvius near Ironton and is one of the few complete stacks standing in the region.

69

Lake

A 1949 article in Ironton Tribune described Lake Vesuvius as "a recreational area whose scenic beauty is unsurpassed." The hundreds of thousands of visitors since 1939 no doubt agree with that statement.

Lake Vesuvius was constructed around the old Vesuvius Furnace property. It is located within Wayne National Forest and offers plenty of outdoor activities for everyone.

Many postcards advertising the lake's beauty and activities offered were produced since 1939. I have added what I could find to this book, but I'm certain many others are out there and will be added to an updated edition of this book in the future.

A group of lake explorers paddle along Lake Vesuvius in this postcard view from the 1940s. The following page layout, shows the lakes's spillway as well as the beautiful surrounds common in the area.

SPILL-WAY AT LAKE VESUVIUS, IRONTON, OHIO

View of Vesuvius Lake from Spillway, Ironton, Ohio

"The Dream Lake of Ironton"

VIEW OF LAKE VESUVIUS, IRONTON, OHIO

BATHING BEACH AT LAKE VESUVIUS, IRONTON, OHIO

A postcard view of the old beach area at Lake Vesuvius. Today the lake offers many activities that shows off the areas natural beauty and charm.

A rare postcard view of the 26 acre Lawco Lake in Pedro Ohio. The lake has provided many pleasant memories for those that have stayed at the cabins throughout the years.

LAWCO LAKE, IRONTON, OHIO

Parks

Sadly, many parks that once dotted area have disappeared as people have become interested with more indoor activities. As fewer and fewer visited the parks, money for park maintenance dried up which in turn caused park closures. It happens.

If it wasn't for park postcards from our past, I don't think we would have known that some of these areas existed. I have several postcards of Ironton area parks that have faded into the mists of time. That was a time when people visited these areas as a way to unwind and enjoy some social interaction.

Of the cards that I possess, I know of only Beechwood Park in existence today. It is near the high school and university, just off of U.S. 52.

A 1910 postcard view of Riverview Park which once was located by the Ohio River.

The grand stand is visible in this 1914 postcard view of Beechwood Park.

Another 1910s view of Beechwood Park. This was no doubt a postcard meant to be used as a form of advertising.

A boy poses on a small bridge on his way through Paradise Park in this 1909 photograph postcard.

Several young girls pose in this color postcard of Paradise Park from 1910. Paradise Park was located near Rt.75 about a mile or so from Lake Vesuvius. Today it is called Balancing Rock Trail and is in Wayne National Forest.

75

A small family is admiring Table Rock in this 1913 postcard view.

A 1915 view of Balancing Rock in Paradise Park. They are still viewable today!

A group of young people and a dog gather together in this winter scene at old Lincoln Park.

76

Rail

Several railroads have ran through Lawrence County over the years. The first was the Iron Railroad (Iron Road) which began in 1849 and ran from the Ohio River north to Centre Furnace. This 13 mile railroad would connect around 9 charcoal iron furnaces with markets country wide via the Ohio River.

Other prominent railroads that ran in the county were the Scioto Valley Railway, the Dayton & Ironton Railroad, Cincinnati, Dayton & Ironton, and the Detroit, Toledo & Ironton Railroad.

The N&W Railroad built a depot in Ironton in 1906. Several postcards of it are featured in this chapter.

Page 78: The three postcard views of the N&W Depot are from the 1910s and give us a color view of the period.

The car ferry was used to transport cars between Ironton, Ashland, Russell, and the Eastern Kentucky Railway at Riverton.

77

Norfolk & Western R. R. Depot, Ironton, Ohio.

NORFOLK AND WESTERN DEPOT, IRONTON, OHIO.

N. & W. Railroad Station, Ironton, O.

River

There was a time when young people of the 19th Century knew the names of river boats and their captains like young people today know music or sports stars.

It was a time when the river was the grand avenue to the world. Lawrence County river communities such as Chesapeake, Coal Grove, Hanging Rock, Ironton, Proctorville, and South Point had wharfs that served as doorways to that world.

One of those well known river boats was the famous City of Ironton. It was built in 1880 and would make regular trips between Ironton, Portsmouth, and at times, Ashland.

Other boats that criss cross the area were the Fanny Dugan, Bonanza, Minnie Bay, B.T. Enos, and many more.

This color postcard is from around 1905 but it is based on a photograph taken several years before. Note the ferry with people and horse customers in the foreground and Bellefonte Furnace on the right.

A boat full of Cotton is the subject of this 1907 Ironton postcard. No doubt this boat had many delivery stops along the Ohio River.

This postcard view of Ironton's riverfront shows a river store advertising furnishings.

A towboat passes Ironton in this color postcard from 1910.

A group of steamboats are waiting at the Ironton Wharf in this postcard from 1905. In the foreground is floating logs ready for markets along the Ohio River.

This postcard is from 1906 and shows a theatrical boat. These boats would make stops at communities along the river and put on plays and provide music throughout the summer.

A side wheeler is the subject of this Ironton postcard from 1908.

The Virginia steams past Ironton in this postcard from around 1910. Note the low level of the Ohio River when this photograph was taken.

A rare evening view on the wharf at Ironton. This postcard is from 1904 and the old Bellefonte Furnace can be seen in the distance.

This color postcard view from Ironton's Riverview Park is from around 1905.

A photographer is preparing to take photographs of two river boats in this 1900 color postcard.

84

Eight postcard views from Ironton and area. These postcards range from 1900 to 1910 and gives us a small glimpse of life along the river during that time.

The above is a pano postcard view from 1914 and shows the C&O Ferry, H.A. Mead which ran between Ironton and Russell until around 1915. It was succeeded by the Ironton which provided ferry service until the Ironton Russell Bridge was built in 1922. Below are postcard views of the C&O Ferry activity between the two cities from 1905 through 1915.

86

Schools

The value placed on the education of children in Lawrence County is evident from the counties very early history. Education began in the private homes of families, but eventually community schools and churches shared structures. This was the case in many of the charcoal iron furnace villages that sprang up around the county.

In the larger communities, dedicated buildings were constructed as schools. In this small chapter are postcards from a few of those old schools in Ironton.

Below is a undated postcard depicting three Ironton Schools: Campbell, Whitwell, and Kingsbury. A newer Campbell School was built in 1937. Whitwell was built in 1894 and Kingsbury was constructed in 1888.

This 1914 postcard shows Ironton's Central School which was built in 1908.

A group of young students stand on the front lawn of Ironton's Kingsburg School in 1898.

Ironton High School was built in 1922 and this postcards shows the school as it appeared in the late 1920s.

This early 1940s postcard shows Ironton High School at that time. Today, many characteristics of the old school can be seen among the updates done to the exterior throughout the years.

Tunnel

The Park Avenue (Natural or Route 75) Tunnel was cut around a decade after the city of Ironton was established. Before the tunnel, the only route north was along the old Ox Road or Campbell Drive. The tunnel had a solid top but the sides had to be cleared of small pieces of debris from time to time.

The tunnel drew the curious for many years. People would travel to Ironton just to walk, ride, or drive through the Park Avenue Tunnel.

This is a 1910s view of the tunnel with a very early automobile coming out of the south side.

This is a photograph postcard of the tunnel from 1910. Note the postcard calls it a Natural Tunnel.

A 1913 postcard which is similar to the one listed above. The time this postcard came out, the sides of the tunnel were becoming unstable and eroding.

This early 1920s photograph postcard shows the tunnel after the 1915 updates were completed. The tunnel was widened and strengthened with concrete on the sides as well as above by the Mahl Brothers construction company.

A 1920s color postcard view of the Park Avenue Tunnel. The two hundred foot tunnel was closed to traffic in 1960.

Ohio

Gallia County

Gallia County was formed in 1803 from Adams and Washington Counties. The county was settled by many French and later Welsh immigrants.

Gallipolis is the county seat and is located on the Ohio River across from Point Pleasant, West Virginia.

Rio Grande University is located in Gallia County at Rio Grande. The University was founded in the 1870s.

Bob Evans Farm is in Bidwell and it was from his farm that Bob Evans launched his successful restaurant business. The farm is open all year and hosts the Bob Evans Farm Festival every October.

A beautiful postcard color view of Gallipolis from 1910. The sun is rising from the east on this Ohio River town that has been around since the mid 1790s.

Built in 1879, this stately building served as the Gallia County Court House for 101 years. It was destroyed by fire in 1981.

Today people in Gallipolis know the building as Lafayette Square, but back in the early 1930s, it was the historic Lafayette Hotel.

This is a 1918 color postcard of Rio Grande College. Today it is known as the University of Rio Grande and the campus is now 190 acres. The university can trace it's beginning to the 1870s.

The Silver Bridge was constructed in 1928 and the New York Central Bridge (Point Pleasant Kanauga Railroad Bridge) was completed around 1886. Sadly, the Silver Bridge collapsed in 1967, which resulted in the deaths of 46 people. This postcard is from the 1930s.

Jackson County

Jackson County was formed in 1816 and named after the hero of the Battle of New Orleans, General Andrew Jackson. The county is around 420 square miles and Jackson is the county seat.

Jackson County was home to 13 charcoal iron furnaces. One of which, Buckeye Furnace, is now Buckeye Furnace State Memorial. It is a reconstructed charcoal iron furnace. It is not a working furnace but stands as a life size model of how charcoal iron furnaces operated in the 19th Century.

In the middle 1800's, many Welsh settled in Jackson County seeking religious freedoms. Today there is a Welsh-American Heritage Museum in Oak Hill.

This is a 1905 postcard view of the neo classical Jackson County Courthouse. It was built in 1868 and burned in 1951. The current courthouse was rebuilt in 1954.

Main Street.   JACKSON, Ohio.

A view of Jackson's downtown in the late 1910s. The Apple Festival fills the streets every September and is well worth a visit.

Main Street, Oak Hill, Ohio

This is a split dual view postcard of Oak Hill from 1908. Oak Hill was once surrounded by several charcoal iron furnaces.

West Water Street, Oak Hill, Ohio

This is a 1915 color postcard view of the Soldiers Monument in Welston. The town was named after Harvey Wells in 1873.

This is a early postcard of the old Star Iron Works. These coke fired furnaces began to replace area charcoal furnaces after the Civil War.

Scioto County

Scioto County Ohio was formed from Adams County in 1804 and Portsmouth is the county seat.

The area has been home to steel plants, shoe manufacturing, and a host of small businesses over the years. The NFL's Detroit Lions team once called Portsmouth home under the name "Spartans".

The Ohio Erie Canal ran from the west side of Portsmouth and connected to cities throughout Ohio north to Cleveland.

Scioto County's third courthouse in Portsmouth was built in 1927 and the columns are Romanist in design.

This linen postcard view of the Scioto County Courthouse is from the 1930s. The courthouse was finished in 1927 and is in the Neo-Classical Style.

This is a color view of Chillicothe Street in Portsmouth from 1917. This is looking north from near the Third Street intersection. .

A popular tobacco shop, "The Smoke House" on Chillicothe Street. This is a photograph postcard view from around 1920.

One of three area roller coasters that once provided thrills and screams. This is a postcard from 1911 and shows Millbrook Park's nearly three quarter mile roller coaster.

A 1905 postcard view of a dirt street in downtown Otway, Ohio. Note how small trees lined the street.

Kentucky

Boyd County

Boyd County was formed out of Carter, Greenup, and Lawrence counties. This was in 1860 as the country edged closer to a civil war.

Located on the west bank of the Big Sandy River, Catlettsburg became the county seat as it remains today. It is named after Alexander Catlett whom owned the land in the late 1790s.

Ashland is the largest city in the county. That area was settled around 1799 and named Poage's Landing after the Poage family. It was later renamed Ashland in honor of the estate "Ashland" that belonged to Kentuckian and five time presidential contender, Henry Clay.

This postcard view of the Boyd County Courthouse is from 1914. The courthouse was finished in 1910 and is still being used today.

A busy day in Catlettsburg, Kentucky. This postcard is from a photograph taken in 1919.

A 1915 postcard view of the Gunnell Building and the corner entrance bank building to the right.

A 1930s color postcard view of the Ashland National Bank Building with a streetcar making a stop.

A group of people wait for the opening of Clyffside Park in this undated postcard view.

Greenup County

Greenup County was formed out of Mason County in 1803. The county extended west near the city of Vanceburg and east to the Big Sandy River at Catlettsburg.

The county was named in honor of Kentucky's third governor, Christopher Greenup. He was born in Virginia and fought in the Revolutionary War. Like many others at the time, he was drawn to central Kentucky by land speculation. He would go on to a distinguished career in Kentucky politics for over 30 years.

The community of South Portsmouth in Greenup County was the site of one of the first permanent white settlements in the state. That village was called Shannoah.

A early 1940s view of the courthouse in Greenup. The old courthouse was damaged by large floods that occurred in 1888, 1907, 1913, and finally the flood of 1937 was too much. It was demolished in 1939 and replaced by the one pictured.

This is a photograph postcard view of the old mill at Argillite. This mill was built by the Eastern Kentucky Railway Company several years after the end of the Civil War.

The color postcard below is of South Portsmouth Kentucky and Portsmouth Ohio in 1915. .

106

This is a rare 1927 postcard view of the grand stand at Raceland. This track was the forerunner of Keeneland at Lexington.

A man and child walk along a street in Russell Kentucky in this photograph postcard view from 1910.

107

West Virginia

Cabell County

Cabell County was named for William H. Cabell who served as Virginia's Governor from 1805 to 1808. The county was created in 1809 from part of Kanawha County.

Huntington is the largest city in the county and is home to Marshall University. The university can trace its founding back to 1837 when at that time, it began as a small private school.

The Cabell County Courthouse was built in 1899. There have been additions on the east and west sides over the years.

A 1907 view of Huntington's Ninth Street from a building that once sat along Third Avenue.

Below is a color postcard view of Marshal College's Old Main Building. Note the field to the left or north side of the building.

109

Today this is the location of Barboursville's fountain and park. Back in 1913, this postcard view is of the Main Building at Morris Harvey College.

A beautiful river and valley view of Guyandotte is the subject of this 1916 postcard view.

Wayne County

Wayne County was formed from Cabell County Virginia in 1842 and named after General "Mad" Anthony Wayne who was a Major General in the Revolutionary War.

The county become part of West Virginia in 1863 when the state was admitted to the Union. The county has a total area of around 512 square miles.

Wayne County is the location of part of Beech Fork State Park which offers hiking, camping, boating, fishing, as well as many other activities.

Built in the 1920s, the current Wayne County Courthouse was enlarged in the 1970s to what is seen today. This postcard view of the courthouse dates from the 1950s.

A bird's eye view of Wayne, West Virginia. This postcard is from around 1920.

A street car makes a stop on B Street in Ceredo in this postcard view from 1910.

Above is a 1911 postcard view of a picnic at Camden Park. Many today remember spending time at Camden Park and enjoying a picnic lunch.

Below is a 1930s view of Kenova's Dreamland Pool. The pool provided facilities for picnics, games, and band concerts.

Greetings from Ironton

Compliments of
W. H. LYND,
GROCER,
Corner Seventh & Adams Sts.
Ironton, OHIO.

The End

Made in United States
Orlando, FL
23 January 2025